Hello Sun Moon AND Stars presents

WRITE YOUR OWN STORY!

written by

original story written by Shalini Saxena Breault

illustrated by Emily Hercock

Original storybook is available in English, Spanish, Greek, and French

IMPORTANT: Printing Instructions

Print as single pages front and back. There are an even number of pages, so once they're all printed you can stack them in order and staple along the left edge and your book will be complete!

www.SwanGoddess.com

This story is dedicated to

_____

_____

_____

_____

_____

Hello Sun
Moon AND stars

www.ingramcontent.com/pod-product-compliance
Lightning Source LLC
Chambersburg PA
CBHW042101040426
42448CB00002B/92